DIRECTOR'S NOTE

The Metropolitan Museum is able to tell the stories of the world's civilizations with such great detail thanks to many generous and knowledgeable donors, among them Mrs. Eva F. Kollsman. Late in her life, Mrs. Kollsman identified a painting in her collection that she knew would enhance one of these many narratives. Aware of the importance of her painting of Saint Maurice by Lucas Cranach the Elder and his workshop, she carried out her own research on it in the Museum's Thomas J. Watson Library. Those investigations inspired her to travel to Halle—which at the time she visited was in the east of a still-divided Germany—to track down the painting's origins.

Although Mrs. Kollsman was unable to complete her research, she knew that by making a gift of *Saint Maurice* to the Metropolitan she would be placing the painting among the Museum's rich holdings of works by Cranach, who was second in importance only to Albrecht Dürer among the artists of Renaissance Germany. She must also have anticipated that the gift would prompt further research by Museum curators, who no doubt would be equally intrigued by the impressive saint and would be able to pursue her research to its conclusion.

With this *Bulletin* we celebrate Mrs. Kollsman's generosity and reveal the multifaceted tale of Cranach's *Saint Maurice*. We now know, for example, that the painting represents the lifesize reliquary statue of Saint Maurice, the preeminent piece in the unrivaled collection of relics amassed by Cardinal Albrecht of Brandenburg, the most powerful Roman Catholic prelate during the stormy period of the Protestant Reformation in Germany. This *Bulletin* and the exhibition it accompanies thus anticipate observances of the five-hundredth anniversary the Reformation, which will take place in Europe and the United States in 2017.

When Cranach's *Saint Maurice* arrived at the Museum, in 2005, it was in need of restoration of its panel support and painted surface. Conservators George Bisacca and Michael Alan Miller ably carried out the panel restoration, and Michael Gallagher, Sherman Fairchild Conservator in Charge, Department of Paintings Conservation, removed decades of darkened varnish and discolored inpainting to reveal the saint in all his glory. Technical study also revealed new information that was key to the attribution of the painting to Cranach and his workshop. Working in her usual interdisciplinary and collaborative manner, Maryan Ainsworth, curator in the Department of European Paintings, integrated these technical findings with art-historical research to rediscover the working techniques of the artists involved and the meaning of the painting. For this research she engaged Sandra Hindriks, Slifka Foundation Interdisciplinary Fellow, and they collaborated in developing the concept of the exhibition, in selecting works to be included, and, together with Pierre Terjanian, Arthur Ochs Sulzberger Curator in Charge, Department of Arms and Armor, in writing this *Bulletin*.

It is a testament to the wealth of the Museum's collections that a focus show on Cranach's *Saint Maurice* can be drawn almost entirely from in-house sources. I am grateful to the staff of the Departments of Medieval Art and The Cloisters, Arms and Armor, and Drawings and Prints as well as the Watson Library for their collegiality and generosity in collaborating on this project. The exhibition has been enhanced by select loans from the New York collections of Stephen K. and Janie Woo Scher and from Marei von Saher, heir to the Jacques Goudstikker Collection. It is made possible through the generosity of Northern Trust, to whom I express our sincere gratitude. I would also like to thank our trustee and dear friend Mrs. Henry J. Heinz II for making this publication and so many others possible.

Thomas P. Campbell
Director

WITH HIS REGAL bearing, luxurious silver armor, and large plumed hat, the black soldier in *Saint Maurice* (fig. 1) is a commanding presence among the Metropolitan Museum's significant collection of works by Lucas Cranach the Elder (1472–1553) and his workshop. The whereabouts of the painting had been unknown since it was offered for sale in 1946 at a Parke-Bernet auction, and its reappearance in 2005 caught the Museum by surprise. It had been in various private collections, the last of which was within walking distance of the Metropolitan in an apartment on Fifth Avenue. This fact remained hidden, however, until its most recent owner, Mrs. Eva F. Kollsman, declared that she wished to bequeath the painting to the Met upon her death. Since 2005, when the painting arrived at the Museum, scholarly research and technical examination have provided new insights into the work itself and its historical context.[1] As a result, *Saint Maurice* has now been revealed as an important and complex work of German Renaissance art, produced in the tumultuous years of the Reformation and charged with religious and political meaning.

1. Lucas Cranach the Elder (German, 1472–1553) and workshop. *Saint Maurice*, ca. 1520–25. Oil on linden wood, 53⅝ x 15¼ in. (136.2 x 38.7 cm). The Metropolitan Museum of Art, New York; Bequest of Eva F. Kollsman, 2005 (2006.469)

2. South German Master (active early 16th century). *Saint Maurice and the Theban Legion,* ca. 1515–20. Oil on wood, 26⅞ x 27⅝ in. (68.4 x 70.1 cm). Collection of Marei von Saher, the heir of Jacques Goudstikker, New York

A BLACK SAINT VENERATED IN A GERMAN ARCHDIOCESE

According to the *Passio Acaunensium martyrum* (*The Passion of the Martyrs of Agaunum*), written between 443 and 450 by Eucherius (d. 450), the bishop of Lyons, Mauritius (known today as Maurice) was a native of Thebes, Egypt, who became a high-ranking officer in the Roman army in the third century (fig. 2). The legion he commanded was composed entirely of Christians. Normally deployed in the East, he and his soldiers were sent from Egypt to the West to assist Emperor Maximian (ca. 250–ca. 310) in a campaign against the insurgent Gauls. When Maximian gave the order to persecute the Christians there, Maurice and his legionnaires refused and moved their camp to Agaunum (present-day Saint-Maurice-en-Valais, in southwestern Switzerland). Even after the emperor retaliated twice by decimating the legion's ranks, Maurice and his remaining companions did not obey. Although they respected military orders, the soldiers would not renounce their Christian faith. Maximian, demanding unconditional obedience, thereupon had the entire Theban Legion executed.

The authenticity of the legend of the martyrdom of Saint Maurice and his companions has been much debated.[2] A second, anonymous account, chronicled between 475 and 500, differs from Eucherius's version in claiming that Maurice and his soldiers suffered martyrdom for refusing to worship the Roman gods.[3]

The cult of Saint Maurice was first associated with the royal house of Burgundy in the sixth century. In 515, in Valais, Sigismund, the Burgundian prince who would become king in 516, established a basilica and a monastery to accommodate the masses of devotees who thronged there.[4] In the tenth century, the cult was further promoted by the Ottonian dynasty, which introduced the veneration of the saint into their Saxon territories. Otto the Great (912–973), king of the Germans from 936 and Holy Roman Emperor from 962, manifested a deep reverence for Maurice and made him his personal patron. He established the saint's cult in his new imperial residence at Magdeburg, founding there a monastery, a church, and an archiepiscopal see (a group of churches under a bishop's jurisdiction) around the relics of Maurice, which he had been able to obtain in 961.[5] Otto designated the Theban martyr as patron not only of Magdeburg but also of the Holy Roman Empire. From the mid-twelfth century (as far as is documented) until the sixteenth, the emperor was anointed at the altar of Saint Maurice in Saint Peter's Basilica in Rome.[6] The saint's cult subsequently was featured prominently within the emperor's coronation ritual by one of the imperial insignia, the Holy Lance (also known as the Longinus Lance; fig. 3). One of the most revered relics in Christianity, as it was believed to have inflicted Christ's death wound, the lance was declared by Otto to have been Maurice's personal weapon.

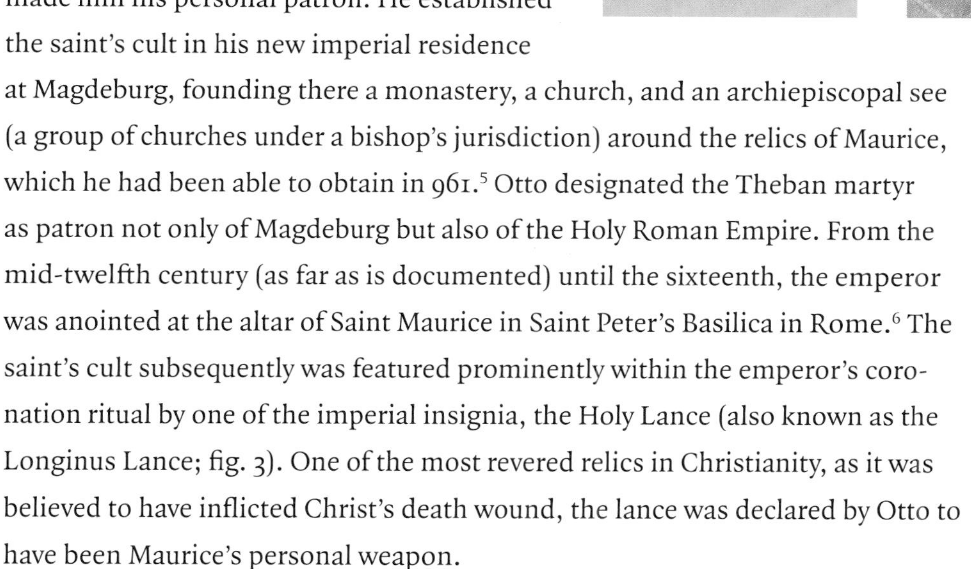

3. The Holy Lance. Head of lance: steel, iron, brass, leather, silver, and gold, L. 20 in. (50.7 cm). Imperial Treasury, Hofburg Palace, Vienna (WS XIII 19)

4. Unknown German artist. *Saint Maurice*, ca. 1240–50. Polychromed limestone, H. 45¼ in. (115 cm). Cathedral of Saint Maurice and Saint Catherine, Magdeburg, Germany

Hailing from a remote corner of the Roman Empire that was populated by blacks and also representing the virtues of the perfect Christian warrior, Maurice was ideally suited to epitomize the contemporary ambitions to expand Christian rule. In the first half of the thirteenth century—at a time when the archbishops of Magdeburg strove to extend their territories eastward to the pagan Slavic lands across the Elbe—this symbolic potential may have led to a startling iconographic innovation: the appearance of a black Saint Maurice.[7] As early as the twelfth century, Maurice had been described as "the leader of the Moors" in the German *Kaiserchronik*, a widely read chronicle of emperors compiled in Regensburg about

1160.[8] To judge from surviving works of art, however, it appears that knowledge of the saint's African descent did not find a corresponding visual representation before the thirteenth century.

In the sculptural program of the newly built cathedral of Magdeburg, undertaken between 1240 and 1250, the martyr was for the first time depicted as a black saint, with features that were thought of as African (fig. 4).[9] This new portrayal was remarkable because blackness in the earlier Middle Ages had often been associated with negative connotations, symbolizing evil, sin, and the demonic. The transformation might have been fostered by a changing perception that developed in the late twelfth and early thirteenth centuries under the reign of the

5. Workshop of Lucas Cranach the Elder. *Cardinal Albrecht of Brandenburg*, after 1529. Oil on wood, 21 x 15⅞ in. (53.4 x 40.2 cm). Jagdschloss Grunewald, Berlin

6. Neues Stift, Dominican Church, Halle

German Hohenstaufen dynasty. Holy Roman Emperor Friedrich II (1194–1250), a member of that family, employed numerous dark-skinned musicians, servants, soldiers, and advisers in his entourage as a way of signifying his claim to world dominion. His magnificent ceremonial processions, in which Africans appeared not as slaves but as court retainers, helped to accustom Europeans to the characteristic appearance of foreigners and to define a more positive image of black individuals. This created a climate favorable for the advent of the black Saint Maurice.[10] It has been suggested that the emperor's command may have been responsible for Maurice's portrayal as black in Magdeburg, but this hypothesis has been challenged by scholars who believe that Friedrich cherished no particular interest in the city and that his court would have had only an indirect influence in the matter.[11]

This new iconography never gained universal acceptance but remained a local phenomenon. Initiated in Magdeburg, where the martyr's relics were enshrined, it did not spread much beyond the sphere of influence of that archdiocese.[12] Within the ecclesiastical province, however, the image of the black Maurice enjoyed wide popularity into the sixteenth century, and thus the search for the original location of Cranach's *Saint Maurice* should begin there.

ALBRECHT OF BRANDENBURG'S NEUES STIFT

At the time Lucas Cranach the Elder and his workshop painted *Saint Maurice*, about 1520–25, the archdiocese of Magdeburg was ruled by Albrecht of Brandenburg (1490–1545; fig. 5), one of the most influential and wealthy individuals within the German realm. The youngest son of a family of Wettin and Habsburg descent,

Albrecht had accumulated an unparalleled number of ecclesiastical offices and benefices. In 1513, at the age of twenty-three, he was elected archbishop of Magdeburg and administrator of the bishopric of Halberstadt; a year later, he obtained the electorate of Mainz and succeeded as high chancellor primate. His quick rise in the church hierarchy reached its peak in 1518, when he was appointed cardinal and thereby became the most powerful prelate in the Holy Roman Empire.[13] Albrecht's stature and influence arose not only from his titles but also from his landholdings. During the Renaissance period in Germany, the principalities that constituted the Holy Roman Empire were ruled by Catholic prelates who lived in the sumptuous style of princes. Albrecht of Brandenburg enjoyed such privileges, which continued in part because of his close relationship with Charles V (1500–1558), Holy Roman Emperor.

Recognizing that a smaller city offered him greater possibilities to realize his ambitions, Albrecht took up his permanent residence in nearby Halle rather than in Magdeburg. His predecessor, Ernst of Wettin (1464–1513), archbishop of Magdeburg from 1476 to 1513, had already built a castle in Halle that was named for Saint Maurice. The so-called Moritzburg was completed by 1503 and became the main residence of both rulers.[14] Immediately after his accession, in 1513, Albrecht succeeded in a project his predecessor had failed to realize, namely, the transformation of the castle's chapel into a collegiate church.[15] Such churches, maintained by a college of canons in a nonmonastic community of clergy, were self-governing, much like a cathedral, and usually were surrounded by large, church-owned landholdings.

While Ernst of Wettin had been a notable art patron and ardent collector of relics, even he was surpassed by his successor, whose treasury soon proved too extensive for the Moritzburg church. It was not until 1518, however, after his appointment as cardinal, that Albrecht obtained papal permission to transfer his collegiate foundation to a larger, more representative church.[16] Taking over the nearby Dominican church (fig. 6), the archbishop set about installing his Neues Stift (New Foundation), which was dedicated in 1523 to Saint Maurice, Saint Mary Magdalen, and Saint Erasmus. Since the collegiate church was intended as a showplace for both Albrecht's relic collection and his art patronage, it was entirely renovated in accordance with an elaborate decorative program. It is in the context of the Neues Stift that the Museum's *Saint Maurice* finds its origin.

From about 1520 to 1525, Albrecht employed Lucas Cranach to design sixteen large-scale altarpieces for his church in Halle. The altarpieces were probably commissioned about the time of the official foundation of the collegiate church, on June 28, 1520.[17] Whether they were completed upon the dedication of the Neues

Stift in 1523 is unknown, but they must have been installed by October 1525, when they were listed in a detailed inventory of the church's possessions.

This extensive Saints and Passion cycle, comprising more than 142 panels, could not have been carried out by one artist alone. Lucas Cranach the Elder, whose fame was surpassed in Germany only by Albrecht Dürer's, had worked since 1505 as court painter to the Saxon Elector Friedrich III, the Wise (1463–1525; fig. 7), and had established a prolific workshop with numerous pupils and assistants in Wittenberg. Renowned as *pictor celerrimus* (the fastest painter), he was capable of handling large commissions and had a reputation for completing them on time.[18] Although the altarpieces of the Neues Stift have survived only in a fragmentary state, their original placement and iconographic program are known from the detailed inventory of 1525 as well as from models and preparatory drawings.[19] In addition to multiple panels, the ensembles occasionally had more than one means of opening them. While the central panels depicted episodes from Christ's Passion, the wings usually presented standing saints on both the interior and exterior. Maurice's status as patron saint of the Neues Stift makes it highly likely that the Museum's painting was included among these works. Its narrow

7, 8. Lucas Cranach the Elder. *Friedrich III (1463–1525), the Wise, Elector of Saxony* and *Johann I (1468–1532), the Constant, Elector of Saxony*, 1533 and 1532–33. Each: oil on wood, with two affixed paper labels, 8 x 5⅝ in. (20.3 x 14.3 cm). The Metropolitan Museum of Art, New York; Gift of Robert Lehman, 1946 (46.179.1, .2)

9. *Saint Maurice*, before cleaning

format and the depiction of the figure as facing to the right suggest that the panel formed the interior left wing of one of the altarpieces, the remainder of which probably no longer exists.

RESTORATION AND TECHNICAL INVESTIGATION

When *Saint Maurice* arrived at the Museum, late in 2005, it was obvious that the linden panel on which it was made was in need of repair, but initially its exact state and condition were unclear because a dense veil of accumulated grime as well as a grossly discolored varnish obscured its surface (fig. 9). The subsequent panel work carried out by conservators George Bisacca and Michael Alan Miller and the cleaning and restoration undertaken by Michael Gallagher, Sherman Fairchild Conservator in Charge of the Department of Paintings Conservation, revealed a marvelously intact and quite impressive armored black saint (compare figs. 1 and 9).

With the cleaning and restoration of the picture, its details could be studied more effectively, and the question of its authorship could be properly addressed. Was the painting entirely by Cranach's own hand, or did he engage assistants to help carry out the work? Given the time pressure—just five years—under which sixteen altarpieces were to be produced for the Neues Stift, Cranach clearly was obliged to rely on workshop assistants to complete the project. Trained in Cranach's style, these assistants had to deliver work at a level of quality that met with his approval. The division of labor between the master and his assistants within any given work can often be clarified by technical examinations that disclose details of handling and execution.

Infrared reflectography of *Saint Maurice*, which shows the artist's initial sketch or underdrawing on the panel, reveals the marvelously sensitive and pensive expression of the face; the spontaneous, free drawing in brush and a liquid medium of the ostrich feathers on the hat; and the deft execution of the main features of the armor, sword, and banner (figs. 10, 13). Interestingly, quite a number of features of the armor were not underdrawn but were added in a late paint stage, and certain adjustments were made from the underdrawing to the final painted form. Among the details added later in paint were the gilt badges of the Order of the

10, 11. Infrared reflectograms: details of underdrawings of *Saint Maurice* (left) and *The Martyrdom of Saint Barbara* (right; see fig. 12)

12. Lucas Cranach the Elder. *The Martyrdom of Saint Barbara*, ca. 1510. Oil on wood, overall 60⅜ x 54¼ in. (153.4 x 137.8 cm). The Metropolitan Museum of Art, New York; Rogers Fund, 1957 (57.22)

13, 14. *Saint Maurice,* detail of armor and banner: infrared reflectogram (left); painting (right)

15. Lucas Cranach. *Judith with the Head of Holofernes,* ca. 1530. Oil on wood, 35¼ x 24⅜ in. (89.5 x 61.9 cm). The Metropolitan Museum of Art, New York; Rogers Fund, 1911 (11.15)

Golden Fleece, Emperor Charles V's insignia, on the breastplate and pauldrons (shoulder defenses); many of the jewels on the armor's elements and the grip of the sword were also newly added in the paint layers, having been only summarily suggested in the underdrawing. Furthermore, the underdrawn flutes adorning the breastplate conformed to the convex form of the chest, while the painted ones do not. The drawing of the plates of the fauld (skirt) also acknowledged their rounded form, but the painter produced these as straight lines (figs. 13, 14). These differences indicate that the draftsman had a better understanding and a more sophisticated approach to the execution of form than the artist who carried out the design in paint.

The question of the attribution of the painting can be further investigated by comparing it with works reliably attributed to Cranach, such as the Museum's *Martyrdom of Saint Barbara* (fig. 12) and *Judith with the Head of Holofernes* (fig. 15). The same spontaneity and directness of approach seen in the underdrawing of *Saint Maurice* is evident in the initial sketch for the face of Saint Barbara in the *Martyrdom*

SANCTA · MARIA

(figs. 10, 11). Furthermore, if Judith's decorative collar is compared with Saint Maurice's gorget (neck defense; compare fig. 15 and cover ill.), it is clear that the former far surpasses the latter in the ability to convincingly portray the reflection of light on jewels and gold. These observations support the conclusion that the underdrawing of *Saint Maurice* appears to be on the sophisticated level of Cranach's own hand, while the painting of the saint's armor must be the product of an assistant. It seems logical to assume that Cranach was generally involved in various ways at the underdrawing, or design, stage of the many paintings for the Neues Stift as well as in the supervision of their final painted form, but that he relied on assistants to complete the task of painting in a timely fashion.

The Met's *Saint Maurice* has a doppelgänger that further connects it with Albrecht of Brandenburg. This is the left wing of the intact Marienaltar (Altarpiece of the Virgin Mary) for the Marktkirche in the center of Halle (fig. 16). Kneeling in adoration of the Virgin and Child in the central panel is none other than Albrecht himself. The representation here of Saint Maurice, standing in all his glory, originates from the same source as the Met's painting, that is, the lifesize reliquary statue of Maurice that was illustrated in Albrecht's *Liber ostensionis* (see fig. 26, discussed below). In fact, a comparison of the figures of Maurice, especially the heads, in the drawing and in the Marktkirche painting (figs. 17, 18) shows similarities that led one scholar to suggest that they were possibly by the same artist, perhaps Simon Franck, an assistant in Cranach's workshop.[20] This painter was not, however, the same as the one who completed the Met's *Maurice*.

16. Follower of Lucas Cranach the Elder (Simon Franck?). Marienaltar, Marktkirche, Halle

17, 18. Details of *Reliquary Statue of Saint Maurice*, from the *Liber ostensionis* (see fig. 26), and left wing of the Marienaltar (see fig. 16)

19–23. Lucas Cranach the Elder. Five prints from the *Wittenberger Heiltumsbuch* (Wittenberg Book of Relics), 1509 (all on one mat board). Woodcuts on paper. From left to right: *Reliquary with Adam and Eve*, sheet: 5¼ x 2⅝ in. (13.3 x 6.8 cm); *Golden Reliquary with the Tree of Jesse*, sheet: 4¾ x 3⅛ in. (12.2 x 8 cm); *Silver Statuette of an Angel Playing the Harp*, sheet: 5⅛ x 3½ in. (13 x 9 cm); *Silver-Gilt Pacifical with a Crucifixion*, sheet: 5¼ x 2⅝ in. (13.3 x 6.7 cm); *Reliquary with a Pietà*, sheet: 5⅜ x 2⅝ in. (13.5 x 6.7 cm). The Metropolitan Museum of Art, New York; Harris Brisbane Dick Fund, 1927 (27.54.65, .64, .32, .67, .70)

The physiognomies of the two saints are quite different, and the Met's is far more sensitively rendered, perhaps by Cranach himself. Therefore, at least two altarpieces that depicted the same figure of Saint Maurice were produced for Albrecht: the one including the Museum's painting, most likely part of Albrecht's commission for the Neues Stift, and the other, the Marktkirche Marienaltar.

BUILDING A RELIQUARY COLLECTION

In addition to the altarpieces painted by Cranach and his workshop, the Neues Stift housed Albrecht of Brandenburg's sacred treasures. In a short period of time, the archbishop expanded the relic collection of his predecessor to one of the largest in northern Europe: by 1520, it included a staggering 8,133 relic particles and 42 entire bodies.[21] Although Albrecht's passion for assembling holy things must have resulted in part from a pious awareness of the human need for divine grace, it also clearly reflected his princely ambition. By accumulating important collections of relics, this equivalent of a "prince" of the church was able not only to make himself known but also to emphasize the God-given legitimacy of his earthly reign.[22]

Three decades earlier and in close vicinity to Halle, Friedrich the Wise, Elector of Saxony, had passionately begun to enlarge the prestigious relic collection he had inherited after he returned from a pilgrimage to the Holy Land in 1492. By

1509, two years after a papal edict ordering all bishops and prelates in the empire to share their sacred treasures with the elector, he had already assembled in his castle church at Wittenberg more than 5,000 relics, which were displayed annually to the public. It was only after 1513, however, that Friedrich's collection expanded dramatically—reaching the stunning number of 18,970 relics in 1520—as a result of an increasing rivalry with Albrecht of Brandenburg.[23] Albrecht's treasury in Halle did not have a long and prestigious tradition, but the archbishop tried to compensate for this lack with the sheer quantity of sacred relics he acquired and the precious containers he commissioned for them.[24] No cost was spared to make extraordinary reliquaries that would enshrine and elevate the saintly bones.[25]

Neither the treasures of Friedrich the Wise nor those of Albrecht of Brandenburg still exist today. Nevertheless, the two men's efforts as collectors of relics and patrons of luxurious objects are documented in the illustrated relic books known as *Heiltumsbücher.* Both used printed books to disseminate knowledge about their collections. Friedrich advertised his treasury early on in 1509 in the *Wittenberger Heiltumsbuch*. Illustrated with 117 woodcuts by Cranach, Friedrich's court artist, it described and reproduced his already large collection of relics and reliquaries (figs. 19–23). The title page, with Cranach's engraved double portrait of the Saxon elector and his brother, Johann I, the Constant (1468–1532; fig. 24), serves as a prominent declaration of the family's pious patronage.[26]

24. Lucas Cranach the Elder. *Double Portrait of Friedrich III, the Wise, Elector of Saxony, and His Brother Johann, the Constant*, print for the frontispiece of the *Wittenberger Heiltumsbuch* (Leipzig: Melchior Lotter, 1509). Engraving on paper; sheet: 4¾ x 4⅝ in. (12.2 x 11.7 cm). The Metropolitan Museum of Art, New York; Gift of Felix M. Warburg, 1920 (20.64.2)

25. Albrecht Dürer (German, 1471–1528). *Portrait of Cardinal Albrecht of Brandenburg (The Small Cardinal)*, 1519, inserted as the frontispiece in the *Hallesches Heiltumsbuch*. Engraving on paper; sheet: 6 x 4 in. (15.2 x 10.2 cm). The Metropolitan Museum of Art, New York; Fletcher Fund, 1919 (19.73.114)

Albrecht of Brandenburg publicized his own treasury a decade later in an even more extensive printed guide. His *Hallesches Heiltumsbuch*, appearing in 1520, featured descriptions of 235 reliquaries and their sacred contents accompanied by woodcuts partly designed by the Nuremberg artist Wolf Traut (1486–1520).[27] Following Friedrich's precedent, Albrecht also inserted a full-page portrait engraving of himself on the frontispiece. He commissioned this portrait from Albrecht Dürer (1471–1528), the leading artist and printmaker of the time, who in exchange for the engraved metal plate and two hundred examples of the print received the remarkable sum of two hundred gold coins along with luxurious damask to make a coat.[28] Known as *The Small Cardinal* (fig. 25), Dürer's engraving displayed a mastery of execution that enhanced the artistic quality of Albrecht's relic book while serving as a challenge to the earlier *Wittenberger Heiltumsbuch*.[29]

In 1526/27, only a few years after the publication of the printed *Hallesches Heiltumsbuch*, a second, much more lavish handwritten and illuminated relic book was produced for Albrecht's own use.[30] Designed as a personal inventory of his treasures, the *Liber ostensionis* describes 353 reliquaries, all but three of which were illustrated with pen-and-wash drawings by an artist in Cranach's workshop. Apart from providing faithful and detailed representations of the original objects—many of which ranked among the most magnificent goldsmith works

26. Workshop of Lucas Cranach the Elder (Simon Franck?). *Reliquary Statue of Saint Maurice*, from the *Liber ostensionis*, 1526/27. Handwritten relic inventory on parchment, illustrated with pen-and-wash drawings; sheet: 13¾ x 10 in. (35 x 25.5 cm) Hofbibliothek, Aschaffenburg (Sign. Ms. 14, fol. 227v)

of the Renaissance—the manuscript revealed that the collection grew extensively between 1520 and 1526. Although some works from the *Hallesches Heiltumsbuch* did not appear (these may have been sold or melted down in response to Albrecht's recurring financial difficulties), the *Liber ostensionis* contained 152 reliquaries that had previously not been listed in the printed version.[31] One of those new acquisitions was of particular relevance to Cranach's *Saint Maurice*.

A RELIQUARY STATUE AS PROTOTYPE FOR CRANACH'S PAINTING

As patron saint of the Neues Stift, Maurice was deeply venerated in the liturgy at Halle.[32] Reflecting this devotion, the church treasury contained at least seventeen reliquaries related to him (figs. 26–28).[33] The most important and extraordinary object in the entire collection was a lifesize silver reliquary statue of Maurice. Designed about 1520–21 by an anonymous artist, the work did not exist long; it was destroyed as early as 1541, when Albrecht, whose passion for beautiful and

27–29. Workshop of Lucas Cranach the Elder. *Reliquaries Depicting Saint Maurice* and *Triptych with the Passion of Christ*, from the *Liber ostensionis*, 1526/27. Hofbibliothek, Aschaffenburg (Sign. Ms. 14, fols. 228v, 94v, 15v)

costly things often exceeded his financial means, needed its valuable metal and perhaps also the gems adorning the armor to cover his debts.[34] According to its illustration and description in the *Liber ostensionis* (fig. 26), the statue housed various relics of the saint: "Your Eminence must also know that in the tall silver Maurice, which stands in the choir in a tabernacle before the high altar, there is a multitude of relics, too many to enumerate."[35] Festively illuminated by thirteen main lamps and seven subsidiary ones, it stood on a red brocade pillow beneath its own baldachin before the high altar of the church. Its gold-trimmed silver armor was embellished with precious jewels and pearls, and its sheen must have formed a striking contrast with the saint's black face, which was probably made from wood or metal. Maurice wore a fanciful, wide-brimmed hat of gold brocade trimmed with ostrich plumes, in accordance with the latest fashion in male dress.[36] Dangling from the tips of the feathers were jeweled, teardrop-shaped ornaments that moved as the air circulated and thus heightened the saint's ostensibly realistic appearance.[37]

30. Elements of Saint Maurice's armor:
A. gorget
B. pauldrons
C. breastplate
D. fauld
E. tassets

Of a type intended for mounted use in the battlefield, the meticulously rendered armor of the reliquary statue (and by association that in Cranach's painting) is designed in a style that was popular in the German-speaking lands during the first three decades of the sixteenth century. Its elements (fig. 30) are comparable, for example, to those of an armor made in Innsbruck around 1505–10 by Christian Schreiner the Younger (active 1499–1529), especially with regard to the fluting on the breastplate, the generally rectangular outline of the tassets (thigh defenses suspended from the skirt), and the decorative, bracketlike cut of the narrow plates of such elements as the gorget and the fauld.[38] Unlike standard contemporary examples (fig. 31), however, the saint's armor was made not of steel but of silver, and it was luxuriously decorated with gems and pearls set within gilt bands along the edges of its pieces and with the gilt badges of the exclusive chivalric Order of the Golden Fleece on the breastplate and pauldrons.[39] The sheepskin, represented beneath the breastplate's upper edge, and the Cross

31. Field armor. German, Nuremberg, ca. 1525. Steel and leather, Wt., as mounted, 49 lb. (22.23 kg), H. 67 in. (170.2 cm). The Metropolitan Museum of Art, New York; Rogers Fund, 1904 (04.3.289)

of Saint Andrew, flanked by fire steels and flintstones on the main plate of each pauldron, are hallmarks of armors made for the Habsburgs, who as grandmasters or members of the Order adopted its badges as part of their insignia (for example, in a pair of tassets made for Charles V; see fig. 32). Holy Roman Emperor Maximilian I (1459–1519) was the first Habsburg to use these badges; his marriage to Mary of Burgundy, in 1477, enabled him both to rule over the extensive territories that she had inherited from her father and to head the prestigious order that had been established in 1430 by one of her ancestors. The badges were henceforth prominently featured on the standards of his troops and the barrels of newly made cannons as well as on armor intended for his personal use. This practice became a Habsburg tradition after explicit visual references to the Order were chosen to adorn the personal armors of Maximilian's son and even his grandsons.[40]

Various scholars have argued that the statue's magnificent silver armor had previously belonged to Charles V (fig. 33a, b) and that he had worn it at his coronation in Aachen on October 22, 1520.[41] After the death of Maximilian I, Charles could not title himself emperor by hereditary succession; instead, he had to be appointed by the seven German prince-electors. Since Albrecht of Brandenburg, as archbishop-elector of Mainz, was one of the leading figures in the proceedings and the subsequent coronation ceremony, he may have been given the armor as a

32. Kolman or Desiderius Helmschmid (German, 1471–1532; 1513–1579). Pair of tassets of Emperor Charles V of Austria. German, Augsburg, ca. 1530–40. Steel, embossed, etched, and gilt; each: L. 8¾ in. (22.2 cm), W. 9⅜ in. (23.8 cm). The Metropolitan Museum of Art, New York; Bashford Dean Memorial Collection, Bequest of Bashford Dean, 1928 (29.150.1d, e)

33a, b. Hans Reinhardt the Elder (German, ca. 1510–1581). Double-sided medal with Charles V (obverse) and coat of arms and royal Habsburg insignia (reverse). German, 1544. Silver, cast, Diam. 2½ in. (6.5 cm). Collection of Stephen K. and Janie Woo Scher, New York

present for his loyal political services. Yet documentary proof for this gift has so far been lacking.[42]

Nevertheless, there are reasons to believe that the reliquary statue was clad in an imperial Habsburg armor, or at the very least a close copy of one. The saint's armor is indeed related to an ambitious example that Maximilian I commissioned for his personal use from the celebrated Augsburg armorer Kolman Helmschmid (1471–1532) and an unnamed goldsmith who was his collaborator. Apparently to be forged entirely from silver, the armor was first ordered on May 16, 1516, but was not completed until shortly after the emperor's death, in January 1519; it was still not delivered by April of the same year, as Helmschmid had not been paid in full.[43] A remarkable drawing, unfortunately mutilated and now unlocated, which is annotated at the back with the words "design for his Majesty's silver armor," provides a likely representation of this extraordinary work (fig. 34).[44] Believed to be a preliminary design by the imperial court painter Gilg Sesselschreiber (active 1502–20) for a statue of Maximilian that would become part of the elaborate sepulchral monument that the emperor was planning for himself, the drawing shows an armor similar to that of Maurice's statue. Both have the same distinctive type of one-piece rectangular tassets and, more important, comparable and equally unconventional rows of gems set within bands along the edges of its elements.[45] The slight observable discrepancies between Sesselschreiber's drawing and the finished armor—seen in the form of the elbow defenses, the fluting of the surface, and the treatment of the turned edges—suggest that the artist did

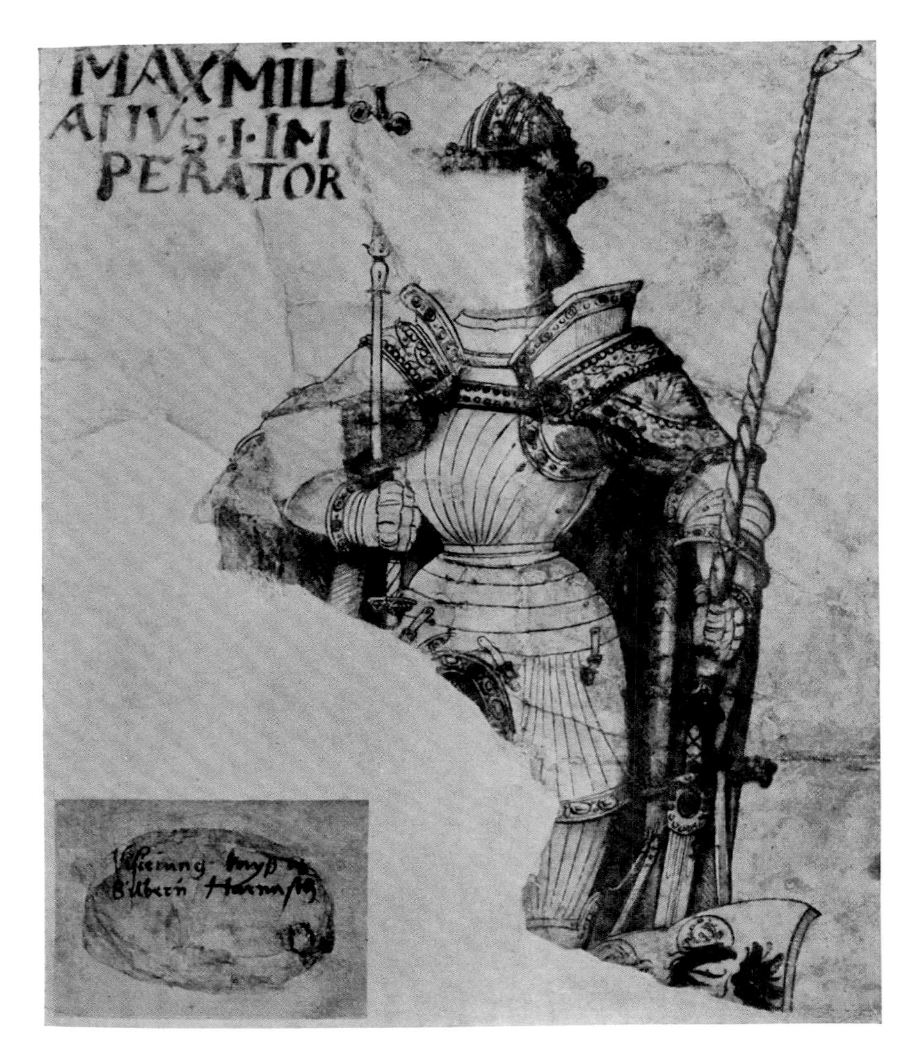

34. Attributed to Gilg Sesselschreiber (German, active 1502–20). Drawing with detail of verso inscription reading “design for his Majesty’s silver armor.” Whereabouts unknown

35. *Saint Maurice*, detail showing banner

not sketch Maximilian’s armor from life, as it was still being made in Augsburg. Rather, he may have relied on one of the multiple and seemingly divergent designs that had been supplied to Helmschmid in 1516 and which the armorer had sent back to Innsbruck, where Sesselschreiber was working, along with a request for clearer instructions.[46] Because the available documentary evidence does not mention another silver armor for Maximilian, Charles, or any other member of the House of Habsburg, it seems probable that the statue’s luxurious armor, which was made of the same precious material, decorated with Habsburg insignia, and similarly adorned with gems, was either the one that Helmschmid had recently made or perhaps a replica.

The reference to a Habsburg emperor is strengthened by the banner attached to the saint’s lance, which is only partially visible in Cranach’s painting (fig. 35) but is fully depicted in the illustration of the reliquary statue in the *Liber ostensionis* (see fig. 26). By featuring the fire steels and flintstones of the Golden Fleece next to the otherwise conventional imperial eagle, the banner identifies Maurice, in both the reliquary statue and Cranach's painting, as the patron saint not only of Albrecht's Neues Stift and the Magdeburg archdiocese but also of the Holy Roman Empire, headed by a Habsburg. This notion finds additional support in the gilded two-handed sword that Maurice ostentatiously displays with his left hand (see fig. 1).[47] Besides denoting his role as soldier-saint and referencing the instrument of his decapitation, the sword may have been inspired by the ceremonial one given to Maximilian I by Pope Leo X and passed on to Albrecht of Brandenburg on the occasion of his investiture as cardinal.[48] Although not a reliquary, this gift to Albrecht features prominently in the first inventory of his treasury.[49] Together with the sculpted Golden Rose, which Pope Leo had awarded Albrecht in recognition of the foundation of the Neues Stift, the sword is illustrated at the beginning of the 1520 *Hallesches Heiltumsbuch*, attesting to the cardinal's close relationship with both the pope and the Habsburg sovereign (fig. 36).[50] Although the sword is no longer depicted in the *Liber ostensionis* of 1526/27, documents indicate that it was still in the archbishop's possession in 1532.[51]

The alliance between Albrecht and the Holy Roman Empire was repeatedly given visual expression within the magnificent decorative program of the Neues Stift. Between 1520 and 1524, the archbishop called upon his court artist, Matthias Grünewald (ca. 1475/80–1528), to produce a painting of a previously unknown subject, *The Meeting of Saint Maurice and Saint Erasmus* (fig. 37). This work replaced the first episode of Cranach's Saints and Passion cycle, depicting Christ's Entry into Jerusalem, which was subsequently transferred to the wall next to the Saint Maurice altar. Grünewald's famous painting, today in the Alte Pinakothek in Munich, was belatedly integrated into the cycle of the collegiate church and placed prominently on the Saint Maurice altar in the eastern bay of the southern side aisle, close to the main altar.[52] It depicts a respectful conversation between Maurice, seen again as the patron of the empire with Charles V's heraldic device discreetly positioned on his armor (apparently modeled after that of the reliquary), and Albrecht of Brandenburg, portrayed in the guise of Saint Erasmus, the patron of the Brandenburg-Hohenzollern family. The imaginary meeting constitutes a political allegory signifying the close bond between the Holy Roman Emperor and the highest German dignitary in the Roman Church.[53] A few years after the completion of Grünewald's painting, this underlying message was further enhanced by the placement of two jewel-embellished, pearl-embroidered busts on the high altar of the Neues Stift. Officially representing Charlemagne (742–814) and Saint Adalbert of Prague (956–997), the likenesses had already been identified by contemporaries as disguised portraits of Emperor Charles V and Cardinal Albrecht of Brandenburg.[54]

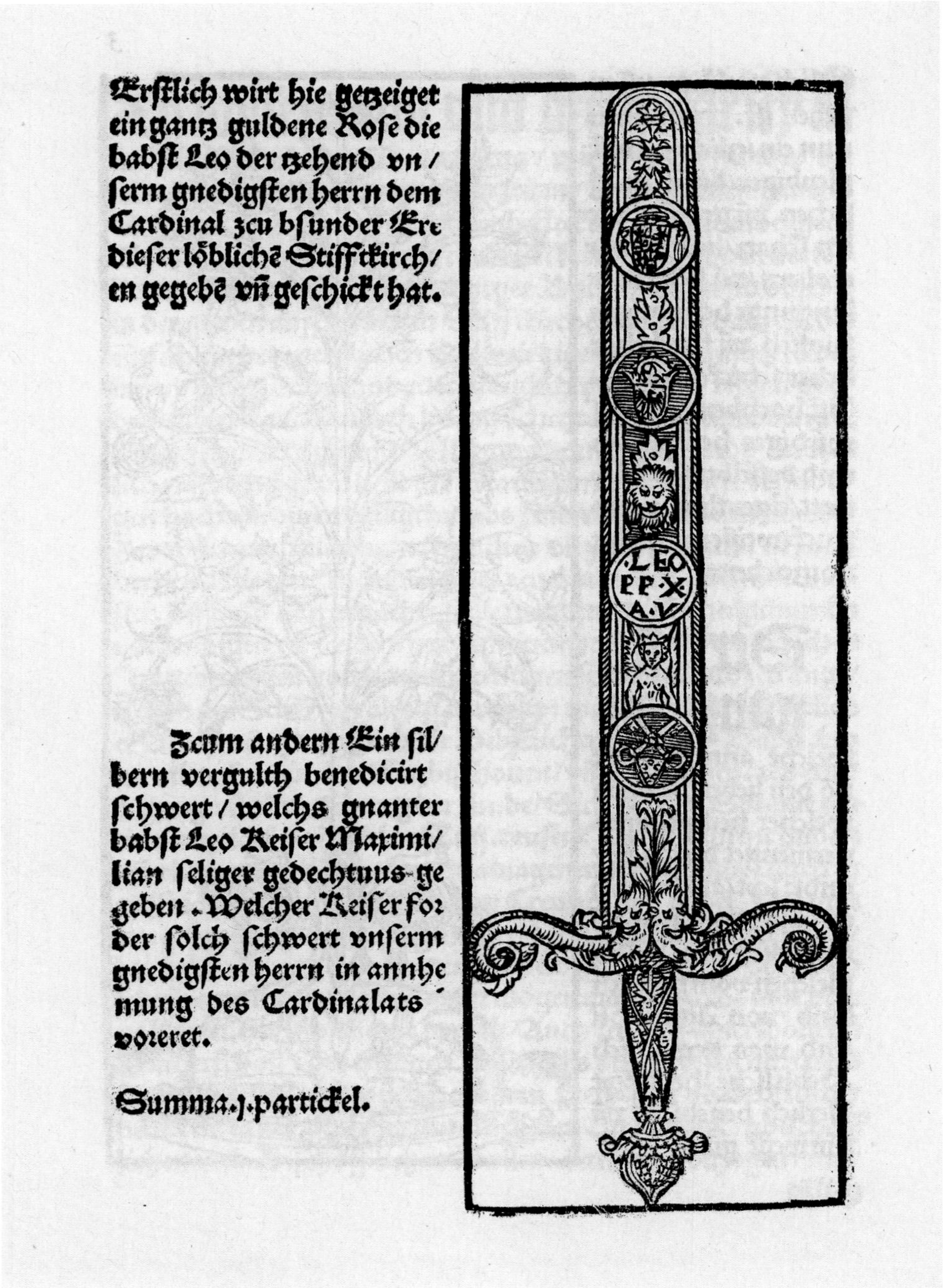

36. Wolf Traut (German, 1486–1520). *Gilded-Silver Ceremonial Sword,* from the *Hallesches Heiltumsbuch* (Leipzig: Wolfgang Stöckel, 1520). Woodcut on paper; sheet: 7½ x 5¼ in. (19 x 13.3 cm). Marienbibliothek, Halle (fol. 3)

37. Matthias Grünewald (German, ca. 1475/80–1528). *The Meeting of Saint Maurice and Saint Erasmus,* ca. 1520–24. Oil on panel, 89 x 49⅝ in. (226 x 126 cm). Alte Pinakothek, Munich

Erstlich wirt hie gezeiget ein gantz guldene Rose die babst Leo der zehend un/ serm gnedigsten herrn dem Cardinal zcu bsunder Ere dieser löblichē Stifftkirch/ en gegebē vñ geschickt hat.

Zcum andern Ein sil/ bern vergulth benedicirt schwert / welchs gnanter babst Leo Keiser Maximi/ lian seliger gedechtnus ge geben. Welcher Keiser forder solch schwert unserm gnedigsten herrn in annhe mung des Cardinalats vorerert.

Summa.j.partickel.

The Museum's *Saint Maurice* was thus part of a grand design and must be understood in the greater context of the Neues Stift, Albrecht of Brandenburg's collection of relics, and his patronage of the arts. The painting also must be situated in the political and religious controversy of the time, for it reflected the archbishop's ambition to make Halle the leading center of resistance to the Reformation. As the most influential prelate in the Holy Roman Empire, Albrecht engaged in a defensive struggle against the Protestant movement, which began and spread from his own territory, in the Lutheran center of Wittenberg. In this

endeavor, he became a close associate of the Catholic Charles V, who on May 14, 1521, placed the Neues Stift under his personal protection while endowing it and the city of Halle with their own coats of arms and generous stipends.[55]

ALBRECHT AS CATHOLIC ANTAGONIST OF LUTHER AND THE GERMAN REFORMATION

Albrecht of Brandenburg's installation of the Neues Stift in Halle between 1518 and 1523 was a manifestation of Old Catholic Belief and as such was directed against the German Reformation movement, initiated by Martin Luther (1483–1546; fig. 38).[56] The collegiate church was intended as a new pilgrimage center of unsurpassed opulence and splendor. Its extensive treasury and artistic riches stood in strong opposition to the views of Luther, who sharply criticized the cult of saints and relics and in particular its commercial exploitation by the Catholic Church: "And though the veneration of saints may have been good in the past, it is now no longer good, like so many other things good in the past and now scandalous and noxious. . . . For it is manifest that the veneration of saints serves neither the honor of God nor the amendment of Christians, but that money and fame are its objects."[57]

Indeed, monetary factors were important in influencing Albrecht's actions, for early in his career he had faced a financial predicament that involved him in a practice particularly objectionable to Luther: the selling of indulgences, which essentially allowed sinners to buy their way into heaven (fig. 39). Indulgences provided a partial remission of the time that a soul was required to spend in purgatory in atonement for committed sins. In the second decade of the sixteenth century, in order to finance the new, extravagant Saint Peter's Basilica, the papal Curia in Rome started a massive campaign to encourage this custom. After his election as archbishop of Mainz in 1514, Albrecht encountered a situation that attracted him to the lucrative indulgences scheme.[58] At that point, he ruled three dioceses simultaneously, in an infraction of ecclesiastical law, which forbade the accumulation of multiple offices without papal confirmation and dispensation. To obtain this permission, Albrecht had to raise substantial sums. He borrowed 21,000 ducats from the Fuggers, a rich family of bankers, who negotiated a deal with the papacy under which Albrecht agreed to permit the sale of indulgences in his territories. While half of the proceeds of the sale could be used to repay his debts, the other half would be forwarded directly to Rome.

In 1517 the notorious Dominican indulgence salesman Johann Tetzel (ca. 1465–1519) arrived in the province of Magdeburg. Buying an indulgence,

38. Lucas Cranach the Elder. *Martin Luther as an Augustinian Monk*, 1520. Engraving on paper; sheet: 6¼ x 4¼ in. (15.8 x 10.7 cm). The Metropolitan Museum of Art, New York; Gift of Felix M. Warburg, 1920 (20.64.21)

he assured his listeners, would forgive all sins and bring release to relatives in purgatory. "As soon as the coin the coffer rings, the soul from purgatory springs" was the preacher's alluring pitch. Infuriated by Tetzel's exploitative activities, Luther felt compelled to protest. On October 31, 1517, he sent a letter to Albrecht, enclosing a copy of his *Disputation on the Power and Efficacy of Indulgences*, better known as the Ninety-Five Theses, which on the same day he also pinned to

39. Designed by Hans Holbein the Younger (German, 1497/98–1543). *The Selling of Indulgences*, ca. 1529. Woodcut on paper; sheet: 3¼ x 10⅝ in. (8.3 x 27 cm). The Metropolitan Museum of Art, New York; Harris Brisbane Dick Fund, 1936 (36.77)

the door of the castle church in Wittenberg. Luther's act was probably prompted by the gathering of people around the Wittenberg church to witness the annual public display on All Saints' Day of Friedrich the Wise's extensive collection of relics, an occasion upon which special indulgences were sold. Believing that human salvation depended on individual faith alone, the reformer opposed the excessive number of indulgences attached to the veneration of holy relics, which had made pilgrimage a profitable business enterprise.

Friedrich the Wise (fig. 40; see also fig. 7), who early on had become Luther's supporter and protector, responded to his criticism and ceased collecting in 1520, shortly after he had amassed 18,970 relics, which were worth 1,902,202 years, 270 days, and 1,915,983 "Quadragenes" of indulgence (a Quadragene being the synonym for the forty days of Lent).[59] Albrecht, a firm representative of the Old Church, still continued to enlarge his collection of holy relics and actively promoted it with a printed guide. In fact, his *Hallesches Heiltumsbuch* was published in anticipation of the annual public display (*Zeigung*) and proclamation (*Weisung*) of the treasury, which was intended to take place in Halle in September 1520 on the Sunday and Monday after the feast of the Nativity of the Virgin Mary. As a memento to take away, the devout visitor could acquire the relic book, which described and illustrated the reliquaries and their sacred content in the sequential

order in which they were presented. Expressed at the end of the book were the absurd number of indulgences—totaling up to 39,245,120 years, 220 days, and 6,540,000 Quadragenes of penance—that the pilgrim could obtain in Halle by viewing the 8,133 relics on display and making a specified donation.[60]

Luther ardently protested against the "idolatry" (*Abgötterei*) organized in Halle. In a letter written on December 1, 1521, he threatened Albrecht with the issue of a treatise titled *Wider den Abgott zu Halle* (*Against the Idol in Halle*) if the archbishop would not abandon his objectionable practices.[61] The publication of the tract was suppressed by Friedrich the Wise's private secretary and adviser, Georg Spalatin (1484–1545), who acted as intermediary between Luther and the elector. Trying to maintain the peace, Albrecht responded to Luther's letter and admitted that he was a poor sinner needing grace. Whether the archbishop actually stopped the exposition of his relics is disputed.[62] No public display is documented after 1521, and the changing attitude toward relic worship may have brought the annual presentations to an end.

Albrecht of Brandenburg and his Neues Stift must nevertheless have remained an anathema to Luther, who repeatedly attacked the cardinal in later times.[63] The reformer finally triumphed over his adversary when the city of Halle adopted Protestantism in 1541. Albrecht, forced to leave the town for Mainz, dissolved his

40. Albrecht Dürer. *Friedrich III (1463–1525), the Wise, Elector of Saxony*, 1524. Engraving on paper; sheet: 7⅝ x 5 in. (19.4 x 12.7 cm). The Metropolitan Museum of Art, New York; Fletcher Fund, 1919 (19.73.116)

collegiate church and took most of its artworks with him; the majority of them were probably destroyed in 1552 in a fire at his residence at Aschaffenburg. A pamphlet falsely attributed to Albrecht was anonymously circulated by Luther in Wittenberg at the time of the cardinal's departure. It invited the German public to a new pilgrimage center to adore some particularly spectacular relics, including "a nice piece of Moses's left horn, three flames from the burning bush, three tongues of fire and one egg of the Holy Spirit, one tip from the banner brought back from Hell by Christ, a big curl from the beard of Beelzebub, a feather from the archangel Gabriel's wing, a full pound of the wind that blew past Elijah on Mount Horeb."[64]

In the two decades of its existence, Albrecht of Brandenburg's Neues Stift in Halle, with its cult of saints and relics and its material splendor, constituted a reaffirmation of Catholicism. The church's extensive, magnificent treasury and multiple altarpieces were a visual manifestation of Old Catholic Belief and liturgy. Sparing no costs, Albrecht resorted to the fine arts and their persuasive visual power to promote his religious convictions. Unlike his opponent Luther, the archbishop never began a propaganda campaign of printed works targeted at a wide audience—a neglect that may have contributed to his ultimate failure.[65]

The Metropolitan's *Saint Maurice*, once included in the collegiate church's comprehensive Saints and Passion cycle and based on its most important reliquary, was undoubtedly part of Albrecht's grand scheme. As patron saint of the Neues Stift, the archdiocese of Magdeburg, and the Holy Roman Empire, the soldier Maurice was perfectly suited to promote the cardinal's self-image as a defender of Catholic faith and to convey his close alliance with Emperor Charles V against the attacks of the New Belief.[66]

That Albrecht of Brandenburg employed none other than Lucas Cranach the Elder to decorate his Neues Stift may seem surprising in view of the religious dispute. Although the Wittenberg court painter was probably the only artist in the German lands capable of carrying out such an extensive painting cycle in just five years, he was also Luther's personal friend and staunch supporter.[67] Early on, Cranach acted as pictorial propagandist for the Protestant cause. Not only did he illustrate numerous writings by Luther and produce many works on Reformation themes, he also shaped the reformer's public image with his widely distributed painted and printed portraits (fig. 41; see also fig. 38). Nonetheless, it seems to have been quite acceptable to Cranach to continue to work for Catholic patrons, including Albrecht, Luther's main antagonist, with whom the painter maintained an enduring professional relationship. Cranach's Wittenberg patrons did not protest against the artist's carrying out these activities. Scholars have suggested that they may even have "welcomed them, at least at the beginning, as gestures that would help to bring about a diplomatic balance," since the confessional distinctions and boundaries were by no means clearly defined in the early years of the Reformation.[68]

Cranach was not the only artist to serve both Catholic and Protestant Belief, for Dürer also produced paintings and portraits for both sides of the controversy.

Early in 1520, when he sent three impressions of his first portrait engraving of Albrecht (see fig. 25) to Georg Spalatin, he expressed in the accompanying letter his sympathies for Luther and his teachings: "God helping me, if ever I meet Dr. Martin Luther, I intend to draw a careful portrait of him from the life and to engrave it on copper, for a lasting remembrance of a Christian man who helped me out of great distress. And I beg your worthiness to send me for my money anything new that Dr. Martin may write in German."[69] The artist never got the chance to fulfill his hope and portray Martin Luther, but in 1523 he engraved a second portrait of Albrecht, which came to be known as *The Large Cardinal* (fig. 42), and a year later produced a portrait engraving for his longtime patron Friedrich the Wise (fig. 40).

Most Renaissance artists, like Cranach, seem not to have considered working for patrons of both the Old and New Beliefs as a conflict of interest. Motivated by pragmatic concerns as businessmen, they accepted commissions from both the Catholic and Protestant sides, irrespective of their own religious sympathies.[70] For Cardinal Albrecht of Brandenburg as well as for his Wittenberg opponents, it was important to employ the leading artists of the time. With the help of the prolific Lucas Cranach in particular, they hoped to make themselves, their ambitions, and their religious positions known.

41. Workshop of Lucas Cranach the Elder. *Martin Luther (1483–1546)*, probably 1532. Oil on wood, 13⅛ x 9⅛ in. (33.3 x 23.2 cm). The Metropolitan Museum of Art, New York; Gift of Robert Lehman, 1955 (55.220.2)

42. Albrecht Dürer. *Cardinal Albrecht of Brandenburg (The Large Cardinal)*, 1523. Engraving on paper; sheet: 7 x 5¼ in. (17.9 × 13.2 cm). The Metropolitan Museum of Art, New York; Fletcher Fund, 1919 (19.73.115)

As for the fate of Cranach's *Saint Maurice*, its fragmentary state—that is, as the left wing of a larger altarpiece—may well have resulted either from Albrecht's precipitous departure from Halle in 1541 and the dissolution of his collegiate church or from the 1552 fire that ravaged his residence at Aschaffenburg, leaving much of his prized art collection in ruins. Even before these catastrophes, Albrecht's most precious silver reliquary of Saint Maurice, on which the painting is based, was melted down in 1541 in Nuremberg in order to pay off some of the cardinal's substantial debts. For us today, this painting documents a fleeting memory of what once was an extraordinary treasury of all kinds of objects—reliquaries, paintings, golden vessels, brocade vestments, illuminated books, and priceless jewelry. But hardly a trace remains, making the existence of the *Hallesches Heiltumsbuch* and the *Liber ostensionis* all

43. Unknown artist. *Triptych with the Passion of Christ*. South German, 1475–85. Mother-of-pearl, gilt-wood frame, silk backing, and tooled-leather covering, overall (open) 8⅜ x 9½ x ⅞ in. (21.2 x 24 x 2.2 cm). The Metropolitan Museum of Art, New York; The Cloisters Collection, 2006 (2006.249)

the more important for the documentation of this once-legendary collection. Consequently, examples such as the Metropolitan Museum's mother-of-pearl *Triptych with the Passion of Christ* (fig. 43), which bears a close resemblance to one recorded in the *Liber ostensionis* (see fig. 29), are particularly important for conveying a sense of the extraordinary refinement and exquisite craftsmanship of the precious objects that Albrecht owned.

Employing the most gifted artists and craftsmen of the day, Albrecht built an unparalleled collection in praise not only of God and the Roman Catholic Church but also of his own power and wealth. Such a pinnacle could not be sustained against the constant barrage of criticism from Martin Luther and the developing strength of the German Reformation. Yet Albrecht remained stalwart until the end of his life. His personal device encircling a splendid portrait medal (fig. 44 a, b) says it all: "The Lord is my helper. Whom shall I fear?" The reverse depicts Albrecht's coat of arms, a listing of his titles, and the date 1526. He

44a, b. Nuremberg Master (German, early 16th century). Double-sided medal with Cardinal Albrecht of Brandenburg (obverse) and his coat of arms and titles (reverse). German, 1526. Silver, cast and gilded, Diam. 1¾ in. (4.4 cm). Collection of Stephen K. and Janie Woo Scher, New York

must have held this medal in high regard, since it was included in the design of his tomb.

The popularity of the imagery of Saint Maurice reached its zenith between 1490 and 1530. It was during this time that northern European artists aimed at a degree of realism, and Maurice thus appeared as a black African saint. Over subsequent centuries, in a growing trend toward idealization, Maurice was less often depicted as a black saint.[71] Nonetheless, the veneration of the saint himself continued to thrive, especially in Saint-Maurice d'Agaune (or Saint-Maurice-en-Valais), reputed to be the original site of the martyrdom of the Theban Legion.[72] Maurice is today the patron saint of the Duchy of Savoy, France, and of the Valais, Switzerland. Some six hundred fifty religious orders dedicated to him can be found in France and various European countries. He has come to be known as the patron saint of the infantry and special protector of armorers (notably the Brotherhood of Black Heads, a historical military order in Estonia and Latvia, and the Italian army's Alpini mountain infantry corps). He is also the protector of weavers, dyers, and glass painters and is particularly venerated by clothiers and milliners.[73] The Saint Maurice of the Metropolitan's painting is not forgotten, but his present-day veneration carries hardly a hint of his former fame and glory.

In the early 1970s, decades before Eva Kollsman decided to make a gift of Cranach's *Saint Maurice* to the Metropolitan, she began her own research into the painting's origins using the resources of the Museum's Thomas J. Watson Library. Mrs. Kollsman's inquiries led her to travel—not without risk—to Halle, then in East Germany, to seek out the answers to her questions. The following excerpts from the journal she kept of her 1974 trip, titled "The Doppelgänger: The Black Saint Maurice," now in the archives of the Department of European Paintings, provides a fascinating look at the heroic detective work and scholarly devotion of this truly enlightened patron.

There hangs in East Germany, in the city of Halle, in a church, a painting of the black Saint Mauritius. Dating back to 1529.

There hangs in America, in the city of New York, in a private library, the same painting. Dating back to 1529.

Once out of Munich, on the Autobahn Munich-Leipzig-Berlin, we were on our way. At a steady ninety miles per hour, we were nearing Hof—border crossing to East Germany and our destination: Halle.

We had warnings from our Embassies, and no visas.

The Embassies were emphatic: you can't wait for visas? In that case, we will not lift a finger for you. We have never heard *your names. You understand? Sorry, Madam. Sorry, old chap . . . Minimum wait for visas: six weeks. We had three.*

Herr Wasser's advice had been different. "Go," he said. "Go and say you belong to the Trade Fair at Leipzig. Luckily it is on, take advantage of it!" Herr Wasser owned a bookstore in Basel, Switzerland, and politically he was far to the left.

Hof. Borders always look forbidding to me, even in the sunniest climes. I feel in limbo, threatened, dehumanized. It was worse in rain.

Halle. Not as I remembered it as a child. Large billboard now: Willkommen zur D.D.R. *To one side, faceless office buildings, utilitarian housing, naked railway tracks. Very new and functional. Church steeples and the old, remembered town on the other. Cutting through it the Autobahn . . .*

We gulped our excellent coffee, collected our papers and the transparency [of our painting] and set off . . . on foot through underground passages which led to the old, untouched town of Halle. Cobblestone streets, narrow. Finally, the old Market Square. At one end stood our goal—the Marienkirche (Market Church as it is now known).

We sat down for a moment by a fountain, to gather our wits and to suppress our rising excitement. One and a half years of research at the Metropolitan Museum in New York, *this obstacle-strewn trip, the nearness of possible fulfillment made time for a moment-of-quiet a necessity. Were we on the verge of an "art discovery," stumbled on by chance? A factor overlooked for centuries? . . . Since both paintings were unquestionably original, dating back to the fifteen hundreds,* who *was the twin—a stone's throw from us?*

Sunlight flooded the magnificent Altar. The left panel—Saint Mauritius. Taller, wider than ours but the same, in almost every respect. It was uncanny. We sat in utter silence.

The appearance of the second Mauritius revived the centuries-old discussion of The Halle Altar and its most splendiferous figure of the black saint.

Our painting—which years of obscurity in our library had left muted and unremarked—had stirred up a hornet's nest. Dr. [Werner] Schade permitted himself suppositions, far-fetched but possible. What if the answer is out of my reach? My qualifications for such a task are minuscule. However, Dr. Schade upon saying goodbye gave encouragement. "You, as an amateur, have the necessary time. Time, which for us, is unfortunately limited."

On the library wall—Saint Mauritius. Ours. I know him better now, but not well enough.

I have met his twin, but not for long enough. Between them lies the answer.

NOTES

1. The information gained from this research was first presented by Maryan Ainsworth in Maryan W. Ainsworth et al., *German Paintings in The Metropolitan Museum of Art, 1350–1600* (New York, 2013), pp. 73–77, 289–90, no. 16.

2. See Jean Devisse, "A Sanctified Black: Maurice," in *The Image of the Black in Western Art*, vol. 2, *From the Early Christian Era to the "Age of Discovery,"* pt. 1, *From the Demonic Threat to the Incarnation of Sainthood*, edited by David Bindman and Henry Louis Gates, Jr., new ed. (1979; Cambridge, Mass., and London, 2010), pp. 139–40, 267–69.

3. See Matthias Hamann, "Die liturgische Verehrung des heiligen Mauritius am Neuen Stift in Halle," in *"Ich armer sundiger mensch": Heiligen- und Reliquienkult am Übergang zum konfessionellen Zeitalter; Vorträge der II. Moritzburg-Tagung (Halle/Saale) vom 8. bis 10. Oktober 2004*, edited by Andreas Tacke (Göttingen, 2006), p. 291.

4. See Gude Suckale-Redlefsen, with Robert Suckale, *Mauritius: Der heilige Mohr/The Black Saint Maurice* (Houston and Munich, 1987), pp. 28–31.

5. See Devisse, "A Sanctified Black," pp. 142–43, 271–73; Suckale-Redlefsen, *Mauritius*, pp. 32–35. Not all of the relics of Saint Maurice arrived at the same time. The skull was brought to Magdeburg later in 1220; see Anne Kuhlmann-Smirnov, *Schwarze Europäer im Alten Reich: Handel, Migration, Hof* (Göttingen, 2013), p. 104; Gottfried Wentz and Berent Schwineköper, eds., *Das Erzbistum Magdeburg*, vol. 1, pt. 1, *Das Domstift St. Moritz in Magdeburg* (Berlin and New York, 1972), p. 83.

6. See Suckale-Redlefsen, *Mauritius*, pp. 34–36.

7. See ibid., pp. 52–55; Jean-Jacques Aubert, "L'insignifiance de la négritude: Maurice le Maure," in *Mauritius und die Thebäische Legion: Akten des internationalen Kolloquiums Freiburg, Saint-Maurice, Martigny, 17.–20. September 2003/Saint Maurice et la Légion Thébaine . . .*, edited by Otto Wermelinger et al., Paradosis, 49 (Fribourg, 2005), pp. 57–66.

8. Kuhlmann-Smirnov, *Schwarze Europäer im Alten Reich*, p. 104.

9. See Gude Suckale-Redlefsen, "Der Schwarze Ritter von Magdeburg," in *Aufbruch in die Gotik: Der Magdeburger Dom und die späte Stauferzeit*, edited by Matthias Puhle, 2 vols., exh. cat. (Mainz and Magdeburg, 2009), vol. 1, pp. 192–201.

10. See Paul H. D. Kaplan, "Black Africans in Hohenstaufen Iconography," *Gesta* 26, no. 1 (1987), pp. 29–36; Esther Schreuder, "'Blacks' in Court Culture in the Period 1300–1900: Propaganda and Consolation," in *Black Is Beautiful: Rubens to Dumas*, exh. cat. (Zwolle, 2008), pp. 22–23, 357; Suckale-Redlefsen, "Der Schwarze Ritter," p. 198. See also Joaneath Spicer et al., *Revealing the African Presence in Renaissance Europe*, exh. cat. (Baltimore, 2012).

11. See Devisse, "A Sanctified Black," pp. 148–50, 276–78; Suckale-Redlefsen, *Mauritius*, pp. 54–55.

12. See Devisse, "A Sanctified Black," pp. 150, 278.

13. See Peter Claus Hartmann, "Albrecht von Brandenburg: Erzbischof und Kurfürst von Mainz, Erzbischof von Magdeburg und Administrator des Bistums Halberstadt," in *Der Kardinal: Albrecht von Brandenburg, Renaissancefürst und Mäzen*, 2 vols. [vol. 1: *Katalog*, edited by Thomas Schauerte; vol. 2: *Essays*, edited by Andreas Tacke], exh. cat. (Regensburg, 2006), vol. 2, pp. 9–17; Friedhelm Jürgensmeier, "Kardinal Albrecht von Brandenburg (1490–1545): Kurfürst, Erzbischof von Mainz und Magdeburg, Administrator von Halberstadt," in *Albrecht von Brandenburg: Kurfürst, Erzkanzler, Kardinal, 1490–1545*, by Horst Reber et al., exh. cat. (Mainz, 1990), pp. 22–29.

14. See Markus Leo Mock, *Kunst unter Erzbischof Ernst von Magdeburg* (Berlin, 2007), pp. 27–32; Hans-Joachim Krause, "Die Moritzburg und der 'Neue Bau' in Halle: Gestalt, Funktion und Anspruch—ein Vergleich," in *Kontinuität und Zäsur: Ernst von Wettin und Albrecht von Brandenburg*, edited by Andreas Tacke (Göttingen, 2005), p. 149.

15. See Mock, *Kunst unter Erzbischof Ernst von Magdeburg*, pp. 178–80.

16. See Suckale-Redlefsen, *Mauritius*, pp. 86, 89.

17. See Andreas Tacke, "Cranachs Altargemälde für Albrechts Stiftskirche: Zu einem Bilderzyklus von europäischem Rang," in *Der Kardinal*, vol. 2, p. 195.

18. See ibid., pp. 195–96; Ainsworth in Ainsworth et al., *German Paintings*, p. 77.

19. For a detailed reconstruction of the entire cycle, see Ulrich Steinmann, "Der Bilderschmuck der Stiftskirche zu Halle: Cranachs Passionszyklus und Grünewalds Erasmus-Mauritius Tafel," in *Forschungen und Berichte, Staatliche Museen zu Berlin 11 Kunsthistorische Beiträge* (1968), pp. 69–104, pls. 6–9; Andreas Tacke, *Der katholische Cranach: Zu zwei Grossaufträgen von Lucas Cranach d. Ä., Simon Franck und der Cranach-Werkstatt (1520–1540)* (Mainz, 1992), pp. 71–169; Andreas Tacke, "Der Hallenser Heiligen- und Passionszyklus und die Erlanger Cranach-Zeichnungen," in *Cranach: Meisterwerke auf Vorrat; Die Erlanger Handzeichnungen der Universitätsbibliothek*, by Andreas Tacke et al., exh. cat. (Munich, 1994), pp. 51–66; Tacke, "Cranachs Altargemälde," pp. 193–211.

20. Jeffrey Chipps Smith, "Die Kunst des Scheiterns: Albrecht von Brandenburg und das Neue Stift in Halle," in *Der Kardinal*, vol. 1, p. 30. On Simon Franck, see Tacke, *Der katholische Cranach*, esp. pp. 41–166.

21. See *Das Hallesche Heiltumbuch von 1520: Nachdruck zum 450. Gründsjubiläum der Marienbibliothek zu Halle*, edited with epilogue by Heinrich L. Nickel, facsimile ed. (Halle an der Saale, 2001), p. 120.

22. See Holger A. Klein, "Sacred Things and Holy Bodies: Collecting Relics from Late Antiquity to the Early Renaissance," in *Treasures of Heaven: Saints, Relics, and Devotion in Medieval Europe*, by Martina Bagnoli et al., exh. cat. (Baltimore and Cleveland, 2010), pp. 62–64, 67; Barbara Marx, "Konkurrenz der Heiligkeit: Kurfürst Friedrich der Weise von Sachsen (1463–1525) und Kardinal Albrecht von Brandenburg (1490–1545)," in *Höfe und Residenzen geistlicher Fürsten: Strukturen, Regionen und Salzburgs Beispiel in Mittelalter und Neuzeit*, edited by Gerhard Ammerer et al., Residenzenforschung, 24 (Ostfildern, 2010), pp. 255–56.

23. For the relic collection of Friedrich the Wise, see Martin Warnke, "Vom Reliquiar zur Kunstkammer: Die Reliquiensammlung Friedrichs des Weisen," in *Nationalschätze aus Deutschland: Von Luther zum Bauhaus*, exh. cat. (Munich, 2005), pp. 46–51; Stefan Laube, "Zwischen Hybris und Hybridität: Kurfürst Friedrich der Weise und seine Reliquiensammlung," in *"Ich armer sundiger mensch,"* pp. 170–207, esp. pp. 182–84; Klein, "Sacred Things and Holy Bodies," pp. 62–64, 67; Hartmut Kühne, *Ostensio reliquiarum: Untersuchungen über Entstehung, Ausbreitung, Gestalt und Funktion der Heiltumsweisungen im römisch-deutschen Regnum* (1998; Berlin, 2000), pp. 400–423.

24. See Christof L. Diedrichs, "Ereignis Heiltum: Die Heiltumsweisung im Halle," in *"Ich armer sundiger mensch,"* p. 325.

25. See Jörg Rasmussen, "Untersuchungen zum Halleschen Heiltum des Kardinals Albrecht von Brandenburg [pts. I and II]," *Münchner Jahrbuch der bildenden Kunst*, ser. 3, 27 (1976), pp. 59–118, ser. 3, 28 (1977), pp. 91–132; Ursula Timann, "Bemerkungen zum Halleschen Heiltum," in *Der Kardinal*, vol. 2, pp. 255–83.

26. For a detailed discussion of the *Wittenberger Heiltumsbuch*, see Livia Cárdenas, *Friedrich der Weise und das Wittenberger Heiltumsbuch: Mediale Repräsentation zwischen Mittelalter und Neuzeit* (Berlin, 2002).

27. One complete copy of the relic book has survived (Stuttgart, Württembergsche Landesbibliothek, R 16 Vor 1) in addition to three incomplete exemplars (one in Nuremberg [Germanisches Nationalmuseum, Hof 135Q] and two in Halle [Marienbibliothek, Schw 7Q]). For a detailed discussion of the 1520 printed *Hallesches Heiltumsbuch*, see Kerstin Merkel, "Die Reliquien von Halle und Wittenberg: Ihre Heiltumsbücher und Inszenierung," in *Cranach: Meisterwerke auf Vorrat*, pp. 37–50; Dagmar Eichberger, "A Renaissance Reliquary Collection in Halle, and Its Illustrated Inventories," *Art Bulletin of Victoria* 37 (1996), pp. 19–36; Nickel, epilogue to *Das Hallesche Heiltumbuch von 1520*, pp. 249–54; Livia Cárdenas, "Albrecht von Brandenburg—Herrschaft und Heilige: Fürstliche Repräsentation im Medium des Heiltumsbuches," in *"Ich armer sundiger mensch,"* pp. 239–70.

28. Dürer mentions the commission in a letter written in early 1520 to Georg Spalatin, the private secretary and adviser of Elector Friedrich the Wise; original document in *Dürer Schriftlicher Nachlass*, edited by Hans Rupprich, 3 vols. (Berlin, 1956–69), vol. 1, pp. 85–87; translated in Wolfgang Stechow, *Northern Renaissance Art 1400–1600: Sources and Documents* (Englewood Cliffs, N.J., 1966), pp. 94–96, here p. 95.

29. See Matthias Mende in Rainer Schoch, Matthias Mende, and Anna Scherbaum, *Albrecht Dürer: Das druckgraphische Werk*, vol. 1, *Kupferstiche, Eisenradierungen und Kaltnadelblätter* (Munich, 2001), pp. 221–22.

30. *Liber ostensionis*, 1526/27, with later additions, 428 parchment folios with colored, full-page illustrations of the objects (Aschaffenburg, Hofbibliothek, Sign. MS 14). See Ursula Timann in *Der Kardinal*, vol. 1, pp. 92–95, no. 27.

31. See Eichberger, "A Renaissance Reliquary Collection," p. 26.

32. See Hamann, "Die liturgische Verehrung des heiligen Mauritius," pp. 287, 313.

33. See Suckale-Redlefsen, *Mauritius*, pp. 216–20.

34. Albrecht mentions the melting down of the statue in a letter written on May 15, 1541, to the chapter of Magdeburg; see Paul Redlich, *Cardinal Albrecht von Brandenburg und das Neue Stift zu Halle, 1520–1541: Eine kirchen- und kunstgeschichtliche Studie* (Mainz, 1900), appendix 36a, p. 157.

35. *Liber ostensionis*, fol. 227v, 228r; translated in Ainsworth et al., *German Paintings*, p. 289 n. 20.

36. For a comparable surviving example, see Eva Nienholdt, *Kostümkunde: Ein Handbuch für Sammler und Liebhaber* (Braunschweig, 1961), p. 39, fig. 31.

37. See Ainsworth in Ainsworth et al., *German Paintings*, p. 76; Suckale-Redlefsen, *Mauritius*, pp. 217–18.

38. The Metropolitan Museum of Art, Purchase, Mr. and Mrs. Arthur Ochs Sulzberger Gift, in honor of Helmut Nickel, 1991 (1991.4).

39. See Ainsworth in Ainsworth et al., *German Paintings*, p. 76. On this style of armor, see Heinrich Klapsia and Bruno Thomas, "Harnischstudien," in *Gesammelte Schriften zur historischen Waffenkunde*, by Bruno Thomas et al., 2 vols. (Graz, 1977), vol. 1, pp. 619–38. Special thanks go to Dirk Breiding, J. J. Medveckis Associate Curator of Arms and Armor, Philadelphia Museum of Art, for discussing issues relating to the arms and armor in *Saint Maurice*.

40. The fire steels and flintstones of the Order, for example, are etched on the plates of a neck defense for one of Maximilian I's horses; see Thomas et al., *Gesammelte Schriften*, vol. 2, p. 1603, ill. Similarly, the sheepskin of the Order is etched on the breastplate of a boy's armor made for Maximilian's son and presumptive heir, Philip, who had been made a member of the Order when he was only three years old; see Bruno Thomas and Ortwin Gamber, *Katalog der Leibrüstkammer*, pt. 1, *Der Zeitraum von 500 bis 1530* (Vienna, 1976), p. 127, pl. 49.

41. See Smith, "Die Kunst des Scheiterns," p. 30; Horst Ziermann, in collaboration with Erika Beissel, *Matthias Grünewald* (Munich, London, and New York, 2001), p. 176; Suckale-Redlefsen, *Mauritius*, p. 91.

42. See Ainsworth in Ainsworth et al., *German Paintings*, p. 77.

43. For a summary chronological overview of this commission, see Wendelin Boeheim, "Augsburger Waffenschmiede, ihre Werke und ihre Beziehungen zum kaiserlichen und zu anderen Höfen," *Jahrbuch der kunsthistorischen Sammlungen des allerhöchsten Kaiserhauses* 12 (1891), pp. 177–78.

44. W. A. Baillie-Grohman, *The Land in the Mountains, Being an Account of the Past & Present of Tyrol, Its People and Its Castles* (Philadelphia and London, 1907), pp. 172–74, pl. 41. The time-honored view that a series of designs made by Dürer for the ornamentation of an armor was intended for Maximilian's silver armor should be dismissed, as it rests entirely on the assumption that because they are of about the same date the designs could only have been intended for the harness that Helmschmid was making for the emperor. Sesselschreiber's drawing strongly suggests that the designs were created for an entirely different work.

45. The idea for the use of pearls and rubies to decorate this highly original and seemingly unique early Renaissance armor was perhaps provided by a late Gothic armor of which Maximilian pawned several elements in 1480 to a merchant from Florence. See Claude Gaier, *L'industrie et le commerce des armes dans les anciennes principautés belges du XIIIme à la fin du XVme siècle* (Paris, 1973), pp. 69–70 n. 28, 81–82.

46. Boeheim, "Augsburger Waffenschmiede," p. 177.

47. For the significance of the sword in the iconography of Saint Maurice, see Suckale-Redlefsen, *Mauritius*, pp. 58–63.

48. Ainsworth in Ainsworth et al., *German Paintings*, p. 76; Suckale-Redlefsen, *Mauritius*, p. 218.

49. *Das Hallesche Heiltumbuch von 1520*, fol. 3v.

50. Eichberger, "A Renaissance Reliquary Collection," p. 24; Cárdenas, "Albrecht von Brandenburg," pp. 261–67.

51. The sword is mentioned in 1532 in the *Breviarius ecclesiae collegiatae Hallensis*; see Cárdenas, "Albrecht von Brandenburg," p. 265.

52. See Tacke, *Der katholische Cranach*, pp. 86–91.

53. See, among others, Andreas Tacke, "With Cranach's Help: Counter-Reformation Art before the Council of Trent," in *Cranach*, by Bodo Brinkmann et al., exh. cat. (Ostfildern and London, 2007), p. 86; Dagmar Eichberger, "Begegnungen: Grünewald im Spiegel seiner Zeitgenossen," in *Grünewald und der Isenheimer Altar: Ein Meisterwerk im Blick*, by Pantxika Béguerie-De Paepe et al., exh. cat. (Paris, 2007), pp. 34–37, 44.

54. The portraits were identified in a poem by Georg Sabinus, who had visited the Neues Stift in 1535; see Redlich, *Cardinal Albrecht von Brandenburg*, pp. 163–65, and appendix 26, pp. 63ff.; see also Cárdenas, "Albrecht von Brandenburg," pp. 268–69; Smith, "Die Kunst des Scheiterns," p. 34; Suckale-Redlefsen, *Mauritius*, p. 217; Steinmann, "Der Bilderschmuck der Stiftskirche zu Halle," p. 104.

55. Redlich, *Cardinal Albrecht von Brandenburg*, pp. 42–43.

56. For a summary of the relationship between Albrecht and Luther, see Bernhard Lohse, "Albrecht von Brandenburg und Luther," in *Erzbischof Albrecht von Brandenburg (1490–1545): Ein Kirchen- und Reichsfürst der Frühen Neuzeit*, edited by Friedhelm Jürgensmeier (Frankfurt am Main, 1991), pp. 73–83; Albrecht Wolters, *Luther und der Kardinal Albrecht von Mainz* (Barmen, [1877]).

57. Martin Luther, *An den christlichen Adel deutscher Nation* (Wittenberg, [1520]), chap. 20; English translation here quoted from Suckale-Redlefsen, *Mauritius*, p. 109.

58. See Rolf Decot, "Theologie—Frömmigkeit—Kirche: Albrecht von Brandenburg vor der Herausforderung der Reformation," in *Der Kardinal*, vol. 2, pp. 64–66; Suckale-Redlefsen, *Mauritius*, p. 89.

59. See Kühne, *Ostensio reliquiarum*, p. 410.

60. See ibid., pp. 432–33.

61. See Gottfried G. Krodel, "Wider den Abgott zu Halle: Luthers Auseinandersetzung mit Albrecht von Mainz im Herbst 1521," *Lutherjahrbuch* 33 (1966), pp. 9–87; John Dillenberger, *Images and Relics: Theological Perceptions and Visual Images in Sixteenth-Century Europe* (New York and Oxford, 1999), p. 86; Hartmut Kühne, "'Die do lauffen hyn und her, zum heiligen Creutz zu Dorgaw und tzu Dresen . . .': Luthers Kritik am Heiligenkult und Wallfahrten im historischen Kontext Mitteldeutschlands," in *"Ich armer sundiger mensch,"* p. 516.

62. See Diedrichs, "Ereignis Heiltum," pp. 328–30; Kühne, *Ostensio reliquiarum*, pp. 435–37.

63. See Mark U. Edwards, *Luther's Last Battles: Politics and Polemics, 1531–46* (Leiden, 1983), pp. 165–72.

64. Martin Luther in *Neue Zeitung am Rhein*; see Devisse, "A Sanctified Black," p. 191, 285; Hartmann, "Albrecht von Brandenburg," p. 9; Diedrichs, "Ereignis Heiltum," pp. 316–17.

65. See Tacke, "With Cranach's Help," pp. 84–87.

66. See ibid., p. 86; Andreas Tacke, "Das Hallenser Stift Albrechts von Brandenburg: Überlegungen zu gegen-reformatorischen Kunstwerken vor dem Tridentinum," in *Erzbischof Albrecht von Brandenburg*, pp. 368–69.

67. For Cranach's friendship with Luther, see Bonnie Noble, *Lucas Cranach the Elder: Art and Devotion of the German Reformation* (Lanham, Md., 2009), pp. 11–12.

68. Bodo Brinkmann, "The Smile of the Madonna: Lucas Cranach, a Serial Painter," in Brinkmann et al., *Cranach*, p. 23; see also Noble, *Lucas Cranach the Elder*, p. 11.

69. See note 28 above.

70. See Andreas Tacke, ed., *Kunst und Konfession: Katholische Auftragswerke im Zeitalter der Glaubensspaltung, 1517–1563* (Regensburg, 2008), pp. 16–17; Tacke, "With Cranach's Help," p. 81; Noble, *Lucas Cranach the Elder*, pp. 13–14.

71. Suckale-Redlefsen, *Mauritius*, p. 121.

72. On the Abbey of Saint-Maurice d'Augaune and its treasures, see Élisabeth Antoine-König et al., *Le trésor de l'abbaye de Saint-Maurice d'Agaune*, exh. cat. (Paris, 2014).

73. Suckale-Redlefsen, *Mauritius*, pp. 139, 141.

ACKNOWLEDGMENTS

There would be no *Bulletin* on Cranach's *Saint Maurice* without the extraordinary generosity of Mrs. Eva Kollsman, who bequeathed the painting to the Metropolitan Museum and inspired us with her early research on the work. We only wish that she were still with us and able to see the results of the present-day investigations and the exhibition devoted to her marvelous painting. We are also especially grateful to Everett Fahy and Keith Christiansen, previous and current John Pope-Hennessy Chairman of the Department of European Paintings, for supporting this acquisition and research project, and to many members of the department (past and present) who assisted in a variety of ways: Rebecca Ben-Atar, Andrew Caputo, Dorothy Kellett, Patrice Mattia, Jennifer Meagher, Joshua P. Waterman, and Gretchen Wold. Dirk H. Breiding, former member of the Department of Arms and Armor and now J. J. Medveckis Associate Curator of Arms and Armor at the Philadelphia Museum of Art, was extremely helpful in early stages of the research on the armor of Saint Maurice. Gunnar Heydenreich, Professor für Restaurierung, Kunsttechnologie und Konservierungswissenschaft am Cologne Institute of Conservation Sciences der Fachhochschule Köln, and project director of the Cranach Digital Archive, generously assisted with many queries concerning the comparative study of Cranach's works.

The painting was beautifully restored by Michael Gallagher, Sherman Fairchild Conservator in Charge, Department of Paintings Conservation, along with George Bisacca and Michael Alan Miller, who treated the panel support; Charlotte Hale and Evan Read carried out the technical investigations. The handsome *Bulletin* issue—its editing, production, design, and photography—is the work of an extraordinary team whom we thank warmly: in the Editorial Department, Dale Tucker, Margaret Donovan, Paul Booth, Christopher Kuntze, Jane S. Tai, and Josephine Rodriguez-Massop, who work under the direction of Mark Polizzotti, Publisher; and Juan Trujillo of The Photograph Studio, who took the splendid new images of the painting.

The exhibition benefited from the generosity of many Museum departments, whose collaboration is deeply appreciated. We thank in particular C. Griffith Mann, Michel David-Weill Curator in Charge, Department of Medieval Art and The Cloisters; George R. Goldner, former Chairman, and Nadine M. Orenstein, Drue Heinz Curator in Charge, Department of Drawings and Prints; Luke Syson, Iris and B. Gerald Cantor Chairman of the Department of European Sculpture and Decorative Arts; and Kenneth Soehner, Arthur K. Watson Chief Librarian, Thomas J. Watson Library. We are also deeply grateful to Peter Barnet, Barbara D. Boehm, Paul and Jill Ruddock Curator, Christine E. Brennan, Timothy B. Husband, Donald J. La Rocca, Nancy B. Mandel, Freyda Spira-Slavin, Denny Stone, and Elizabeth Zanis. Certain indispensable loans from generous local collectors, especially Stephen K. and Janie Woo Scher, and Marei von Saher (with the kind assistance of Frank Lord), have greatly enhanced our presentation. These arrangements were ably made by our registrar, Meryl Cohen. We owe the exquisite design and clarity of the exhibition to the efforts of Brian Cha, Daniel Kershaw, Constance Norkin, Pamela T. Barr, Clint Ross Coller, and Richard Lichte. Its careful installation was accomplished by Martin Bansbach, Mindell Dubansky, David del Gaizo, Patricia Gilkison, Edward A. Hunter, Gary Kopp, Theresa King-Dickinson, John McKanna, Taylor Miller, Rachel Robinson, Frederick J. Sager, Crayton Sohan and his team of riggers, and Thomas L. Vinton.
We are most appreciative to Mary Flanagan in our Communications Department for her expertise, marvelous support, and infectious enthusiasm for this exhibition and its accompanying *Bulletin*.

This publication is issued in conjunction with the exhibition "Cranach's *Saint Maurice*," on view at The Metropolitan Museum of Art, New York, from April 20 through July 27, 2015.

The exhibition is made possible by Northern Trust.

The publication is made possible by the Drue E. Heinz Fund.

The Metropolitan's quarterly *Bulletin* program is supported in part by the Lila Acheson Wallace Fund for The Metropolitan Museum of Art, established by the cofounder of *Reader's Digest*.

The Metropolitan Museum of Art Bulletin, Spring 2015
Volume LXXII, Number 4

The Metropolitan Museum of Art Bulletin (ISSN 0026-1521) is published quarterly by The Metropolitan Museum of Art, 1000 Fifth Avenue, New York, NY 10028-0198. Periodicals postage paid at New York NY and additional mailing offices. POSTMASTER: Send address changes to Membership Department, *The Metropolitan Museum of Art Bulletin*, 1000 Fifth Avenue, New York, NY 10028-0198. Four weeks' notice required for change of address. The *Bulletin* is provided as a benefit to Museum members and is available by subscription. Subscriptions $30.00 a year. Back issues available on microfilm from National Archive Publishing Company, 300 N. Zeeb Road, Ann Arbor, MI 48106. Volumes I–XXXVII (1905–42) available as a clothbound reprint set or as individual yearly volumes from Ayer Company Publishers, Suite B-213, 400 Bedford Street, Manchester, NH 03101, or from the Metropolitan Museum, 66–26 Metropolitan Avenue, Middle Village, NY 11381-0001.

Published by The Metropolitan Museum of Art, New York
Mark Polizzotti, Publisher and Editor in Chief
Gwen Roginsky, Associate Publisher and General Manager of Publications
Dale Tucker, Editor of the *Bulletin*
Margaret Donovan, Editor
Paul Booth, Production Manager
Christopher Kuntze, Designer

Typeset in Quadraat with Quadraat Sans
Separations by Professional Graphics, Inc., Rockford, Illinois
Printed and bound in the United States of America

Front cover: detail, Lucas Cranach the Elder and workshop, *Saint Maurice*, ca. 1520–25 (see fig. 1); inside front and back covers: details, Workshop of Lucas Cranach the Elder, *Reliquary Statues of Saint Maurice* (see figs. 26, 27); page 2: detail, Matthias Grünewald, *The Meeting of Saint Maurice and Saint Erasmus* (see fig. 37).

Photographs of works in the Metropolitan Museum's collection by The Photograph Studio, The Metropolitan Museum of Art, unless otherwise noted. New photography by Bruce Schwarz: figs. 30, 32; Hyla Skopitz: fig. 24; and Juan Trujillo: figs. 1, 2, 14, 33a, 33b, 35, 44.

Additional photography credits: Jörg P. Anders: fig. 5; bpk, Berlin / Bayerische Staatsgemäldesammlungen / Art Resource, NY: fig. 37; Ernst Thomas Groll: fig. 4; Jürgen M. Pietsch: figs. 16, 18; Westend61 / Westend61: fig. 6.

The Metropolitan Museum of Art
1000 Fifth Avenue
New York, New York 10028
metmuseum.org

NOTE ON CRANACH'S SIGNET

During the Renaissance, most artists signed their works with a monogram, such as Albrecht Dürer's famous D inscribed below an A. Starting in 1508, Lucas Cranach used instead an emblem representing a winged serpent with a ruby ring in its mouth, as represented on the back cover of this *Bulletin*. Cranach scholar Werner Schade has suggested that this unusual signet probably symbolized the artist as a rapid improviser holding on to his well-earned pay. Cranach's two painter sons, Hans and Lucas, considered other versions of the signet, but after 1537, when Hans died, a form of the emblem with lowered wings became the Cranach workshop standard.